thunder
and daisy

mercedes paradiso

Published by Mercedes Paradiso, LLC.

www.mercedesparadiso.com

Library of Congress Control Number: 2024915539

ISBN: 979-8-9912170-0-2 (paperback)
ISBN: 979-8-9912170-1-9 (ebook)

thunder and daisy, mercedes paradiso's first collection of poetry, guides readers from the storms of life to the flowers that bloom in their wake. the poems move from heartbreak and adversity to self-empowerment, love, and passion. mercedes believes that strength can be found in pain, and she hopes that you will find your own power in her poems. by weathering the thunderstorms, may you find beauty, inspiration, and growth.

for my family

and

those who have been my storms and flowers

my heart broke
until
poems spilled out

contents

thunder

you showed up like a storm
your thunder shook me awake
i could see
your lightning lit up my eyes
i could feel
your rain washed me clean
i could love
your wind tousled my hair
i could hurt
you swept by as fast as you came
your storm took all i could
see
feel and
love
but you left the
hurt

-passing storm

your shifting energy darkened my sky
you blew in the cold with your games and lies
your silence gave weight to my clouds
and i rain
and i rain
and i rain
words
for you

-downpour

sometimes, there's this thing i do
i run away so i could stop thinking of you
sometimes, it's not you i'm trying to shake from my head
and instead, it's me
maybe in another place
i could just be
maybe in a new city
there won't be the same pain
in new streets and coffee shops
i'll fill my head with different thoughts
there won't be the promises you whispered
your touch
or other precious things that can't be bought
when nothing around me is the same
maybe i'll forget your name

-running

i've saved a lot of "no thank yous"
they're supposed to make me strong
they'll pave a new road
one with shared likes
songs on repeat and
a future that's bright
it hasn't yet come along

i'm hearing it again
the fit's not quite right
oh, you're a dreamer
don't hold on to that too tight

you're not for me, but
you'll find what you're looking for
you'll find it in skipped beats
things not said
when you're not looking for more and
he's in your head

it starts with an expectation
too close to fantasy
it ends with it all
crushing under some
self-imposed
complicated reality

it spins like a record
same as before
i don't know
what is it again
i'm looking for?

-record player

i'm not surprised
you faded away
there's only so much
tapping words in texts
can make me feel for you
pictures sent alone in rooms
exchanging our versions
of a preview
hide your lonely eyes
behind a screen
where it's safe and
the stakes are low
don't feel
or live
or risk a thing
you'll be alright
in the protection of
your phone's glow

-virtual disconnect

birthdays are another ring in the tree
time moving quickly and
a reminder of those who didn't stick with me

i hid in an office behind a degree
kept quiet in a box
to fit into everyone else's reality
but when i'd look in the mirror
who was i in that neatly pressed tee?

stepping into the real me
my planet was small and
inhabitants few
except for a rare native
willing traveler or two

proving to me
with watchful eyes and no likes
most prefer to see me in slacks
negotiating someone else's contracts

-creatives

i can't convince you
the light in our eyes
danced to the same harmony
i showed you
the best parts of me
you peeked but
didn't want to see
don't you know
there is no love
that comes with a guarantee?

i can't convince you
i'm worth the chance
i can give you
that missing romance
the kind that
won't break down
i'll drown in your doubts
you'll take me
round and round
one moment
you'll make me queen
and the next
take away the crown

i can't convince you
we exchanged words that
no one else can give us
that they were honest
true and real
that it's special
the way we made
each other feel

maybe you'll remember
a few things, too
when you're feeling alone
watching old reels
maybe after you bear the pain
of change and
start to heal

-avoidant

you can think about what could've been
that's all that's left for us to swim in

i've seen you change
since you whispered those addicting lines
it's been a while since you've come around but
i can't escape your face online

i wish your image would fade
like you did that day
i don't need to carry it with me because
you could've met me halfway

please take your
podcast voice with you, too
the distance wasn't the issue
it was something in you
keeping us blue

-still waters

we fill the silence between us
with stories we tell ourselves
that make up for the emptiness and
fill in the gaps of things not said
you cast me as a villain
someone you'd rather forget
you crossed me out in red
i can tell by the way that
you left me on read

nights before bed
i wonder whether
my stories of you are fiction
your sadness
swallowed me whole
i became your temporary addiction
trying to make sense of why
you came and went
your character's intent
was it to feel free
for just a moment or
to fill me with your discontent?

-writing stories

we were bookends
with different worlds
to hold between
i'd send you my stories and
we'd meet in a dream

we were lovers of humanity
romance and the cosmos
you'd tell me secrets i'd keep and
give me pieces of you in low-dose

we were two shepherds
who'd meet in notes and texts
we'd dream of closeness
a shared breath
but you plotted a course
so our lines won't intersect

-low-dose

something in me drew you to me
something in my voice
my vibe
the way i laugh when you're funny
you'd never say because
you can't describe what it was

something in you kept you from me
i had that thing you're missing
that thing you keep telling yourself
you don't need to be happy
you made the decision you thought was best
stay the course
never second guess

something in us kept us apart
we don't have to worry about an end
because there was no start
there's hurt and pride
or just another thing
we can't describe

-*missing pieces*

i left because you said it all
without saying a word
you made up your mind and
couldn't be deterred
when i say i don't miss you and
the way you made me feel angelic and sinful
my soul lies a little

it wasn't enough
that we saw something special in each other
you convinced yourself you didn't need anything else
nothing you could get from a lover
when you told me
you couldn't meet me in the middle
my soul cries a little

it didn't matter there was a fire between us
that coveted spark
you'd rather stay alone in your room
with your fantasies in the dark
when i could see
i'd always play second fiddle
my soul dies a little

-second fiddle

you say you don't need the passion of a lover and
that kind of thing is fairytale
but your sad eyes tell another tale

you think my kiss will
cloud your eyes like a veil
but your hungry mouth tells another tale

you worry my touch will upend your life
lead you down the wrong trail
but your trembling hands tell another tale

you fear my love will lead to addiction
inflict pain and cause you to fail
but your lonely heart tells another tale

-lies

true romantics suffer
in a superficial culture
never get to know each other
instead
anticipate the next departure
all hearts are left poor
show us
where's the allure?

love isn't something
to be left on the surface
like a transaction
just another purchase
it lives in the soul level
diving deep down
into the subsurface

confess who you are
be brave enough
to take down the wall
so what if it's scary?
isn't life for living?
so what if you fall?
fill up your soul
you can have it all

-*true romantics*

the concrete of the city turned into the sunflower fields of the country
but it's the forest that reminded me of the dream that haunts me

i don't know why i cried when i saw those trees
from the backseat of the car
but i got the feeling that you weren't just any stranger in a dream
that you came to find me from afar

you walked right through me like you were a ghost
maybe i was the ghost
but you knew me better than anyone ever could
you loved me the most

you kept going and got lost in those trees
like you were on your way to some paradise
i don't know you
but i know i loved you
in another life

-ghost

i can see what's behind your eyes
i know you pay attention to
color
placement
shadows
shade and
tint
with an obsession

you're always
disciplined
dedicated and
focused
on what makes
the best photography lesson

you're good at
painting sexy pictures
with your words
to fill the void
of your love recession but
your only passion
your only purpose
is your work

you dare not get close
you keep love at bay
it gets in the way so
you push it aside
you get lost in your studio
you run and hide

-the photographer

you thought it odd
telling secrets to a stranger
i thought it odd
you calling me a stranger
even though you were
you didn't feel like a stranger to me

the more we talked
the more familiar you felt
the more we got to know each other
the more it seemed
we could just melt
into the same music or mess
or maybe one breath
no, you didn't feel like a stranger to me

you took a step back
questioned yourself
you pushed me away
put me on the shelf
never my lover
whatever it was is over
you're more of a stranger
than when we first met
you're very much a stranger
now, you feel like a stranger to me

-you're the stranger

i could put poems on page after page for you and
you'd still pass me by
my poems would be funny, flow, and
make you feel flirty
i'm standing right in front of you and
you turn a blind eye

i could sing songs for you and
you'd still say goodbye
my songs would be sensual, slow, and
make you feel sexy
i'm showing my heart to you and
still, i'm denied

i could string a million sentences into stories for you and
you wouldn't be mine
my stories would be dark, deep, and
make you feel desire
i'm giving my love to you but
you put an end to our time

-in vain

you're the first thought
on my mind
like you are every day

driving around town
one place to the next
like i do every day
i thought of something
you sent me in text

drinking my latte
one of your videos
came to mind
i saw your eyes
like i do every day
it's how it goes
today is just sunday

putting groceries in my cart
i heard your voice
in my ear
soft
mellow and
clear
it's the last thing
i need to hear

-just go

hearts stuck
stay in a rut
so they reason
try to prove
it's best not to move
maintain the status quo
no need to grow
everything's fine
it's a line
they feed themselves
something
is missing
they're not kissing anyone
something very important
is missing
they're not undressing anyone
something
is very unfulfilling
they shut their eyes and
push away feeling

-denial

i've been hushed and
pushed but
my blood is bold

i've been used
hurt and
refused but
my blood never runs cold

i've been tried
by people i cared about
who hurt my pride
now, i'm tired but
my blood doesn't get old

i've been working
and loving
and trying
in return
the knife of rejection cuts deep
but i keep on writing

cut me again
and again
and again
in my blood
there flows words
there flows gold

-alchemist

i used to drink
more than a little but
less than a lot
a habit but
not enough
to put me in a bad spot

i don't drink anymore
in 2020
i stopped
i realized
what i was drinking for

i was looking for something
i couldn't find
maybe it was me or
maybe it was you i had in mind

you weren't in any sip
i drank more and more but
i couldn't find you in any of it

-*wasted time*

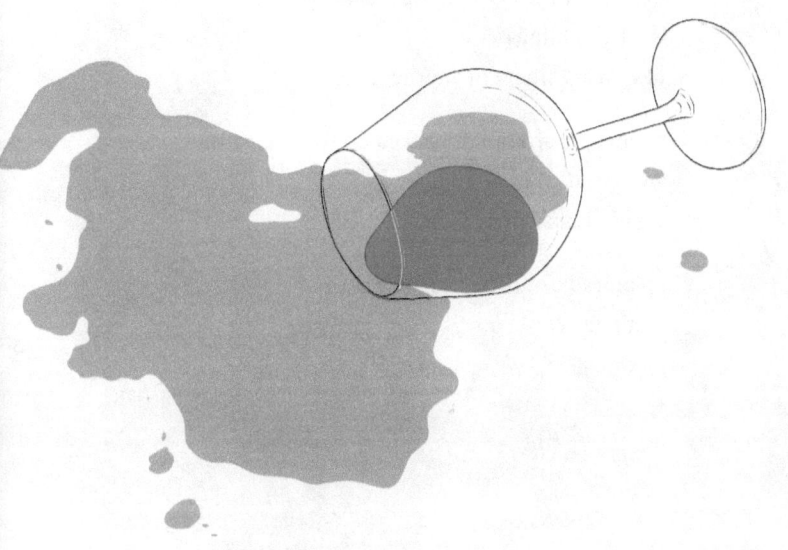

i pictured us on the beach
with our hands on cold sand and
the tide coming in

clouds, heavy and dark
hung over the ocean in the distance
their rumblings
like an argument in another room

the people around us packed up their things and
we stayed still
we hid kisses from them

i pictured us on the beach because
that's all i could do
picture us

-empty beach

you thought i'd be your intimacy substitute
your listening ear
your waiting lady
the closest thing to love in your loveless life
the closest thing to touch in your touch-free fantasy
your guilt-free girl
your willing fool

let me introduce myself
i'm the headline
not the footnote
i'm the elevator to the top floor
not the steps to the basement
the closest thing to warmth in your empty sheets
the closest thing to real in your silicon world
i'm the spoon of sugar
not the bitter tea
i'm the love
not the imitation intimacy

-about the author

you say you need passion
passion you chase but
any passion escapes you

you say you want touch
mind-bending touch but
any touch burns you

you have love in your heart
love lying low but
any love crushes you

you have peace in your home
peace without feeling but
there's no peace within you

you say you don't want drama
vanilla over drama but
the drama is you

-the talker

you thought i was a puddle
you could drop a penny into
my ripples would be
delicate and small

but i'm the ocean
that washes you ashore
my waves froth
rage and
swallow you whole

you thought i was a sparrow
who flies past without a stir
my song would be soft and
quiet like snowfall

but i'm the owl
that holds you in its claws
with vision burning deep
into your dark
armored soul

i'm not the person you thought
you could manipulate
i'm so much more
than you bargained for

-ocean and the owl

an empty cell
i lay in alone
with you gone
the only touch is my own
waking up is the hardest part
you're the first thought
trying to sleep isn't better
i hear your voice
like it's just out of earshot
but it's not
you took your touch
you took your voice
you took you
it's just me
no one to love
no one to turn to

-bedtime

there are a million things i want to say
there are a million questions i want to ask
but i won't
i won't say a thing
i won't ask a thing
i don't have to
your lack of love screams in the silence
your missing feelings ring loud and clear
i hear what you're saying
without you saying a word
but words are all i want
words muttered in frustration
words spit out in anger
words screamed
any kind of words
because no words
are the worst words of all

-i hear you

you drop red flags
like a paramedic drops flares

i make them disappear
like i'm the magician playing tricks

i paint them green
like i'm the bullshit artist

i bury them
like i'm the one committing injustices

-what red flags?

i told you i'd save up all my passion and
give it to you
you said you wanted it but
you chose not to take it
so, it will have to go to
someone else
whoever that is
but until then
your name will be on my mind
when i close my eyes
your name will be all over my lips
when we speak in my dreams and
your name will be in my breath
when i imagine you next to me

-not yours

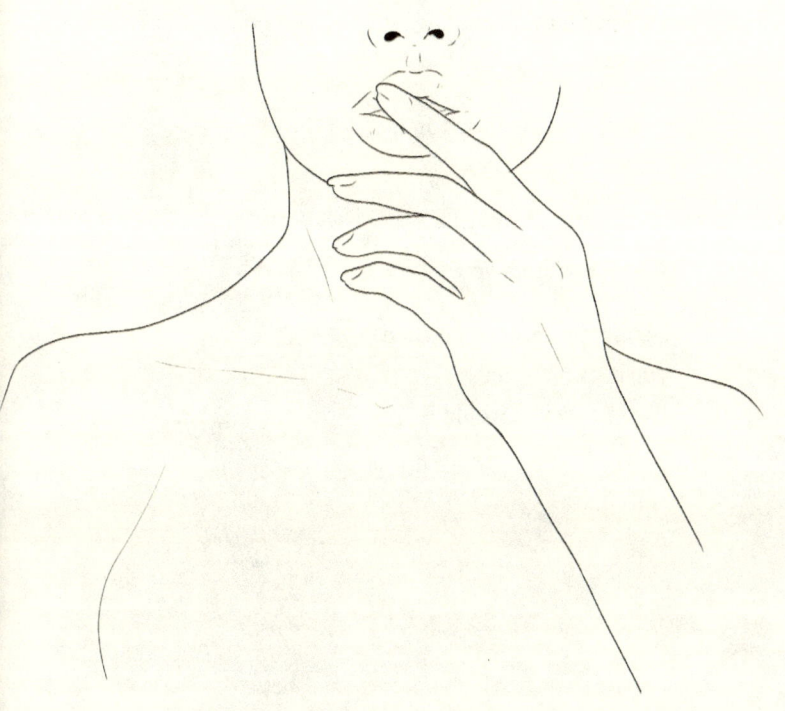

i felt you slipping away so
i slipped away first

i slipped into silence and
i drowned in it

i slipped into my head and
i made up stories

i slipped into my heart and
it broke without you

so, i slipped back to you and
you broke it again
like i knew you would

-inevitable

the first time i saw your face was in a picture
i told myself
heartbreak

the second time i saw your face was at an event
i told myself
stay away

the third time i saw your face was in a message you sent
i told myself
don't go there

the fourth time i saw your face was when you looked into my eyes
i told myself
don't you dare

the fifth time i saw your face was when you stole my heart
i told myself
you idiot

the sixth time i saw your face was when you left
i told myself
i told you so

-intuition

you haven't touched me yet
but your touch is the drug that
will make me weak

you haven't kissed me yet
but your kiss is what
will bring me to my knees

you haven't loved me yet
but your love is all that
will be my downfall

-*contact high*

you come on strong
make me feel
i belong

you know what to say
to make me surrender
it's a game you play

once i'm yours
you disappear without a trace
it's not me you loved
it's the thrill of the chase

you claim your defense
in the name of confusion
but i'm not your addict
you don't have my love
it was all an illusion

-not your addict

you give me love in just the right increments
to keep you on a loop in my mind
to keep me wanting more
to keep me coming back

you know that what you're dealing is just enough
to get me to call
to get me to dream
to get me hooked

when wanting more turns into needing more
your work is done
you take your things and go
but i need that look in your eyes
when we're exchanging smiles

you have another deal in mind so
you cut me off and run
but i need that brush of your hand
on days we practiced with the band
why can't you just give me some?

-the dealer

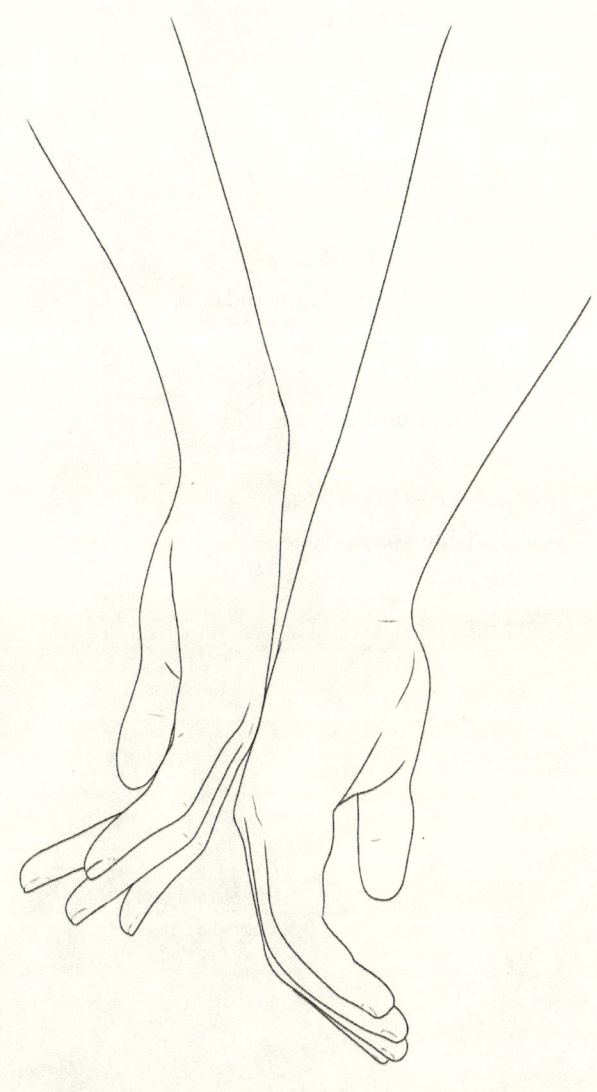

i don't like running but
here i am
in my running shoes
in the rain
feet pounding the slick
black pavement
splashing through puddles and
breaking the reflections of streetlamps
trying to run from the anxiety
building within me
trying to run from the space
you created
trying to run from you but
you're around every corner

-can't run from you

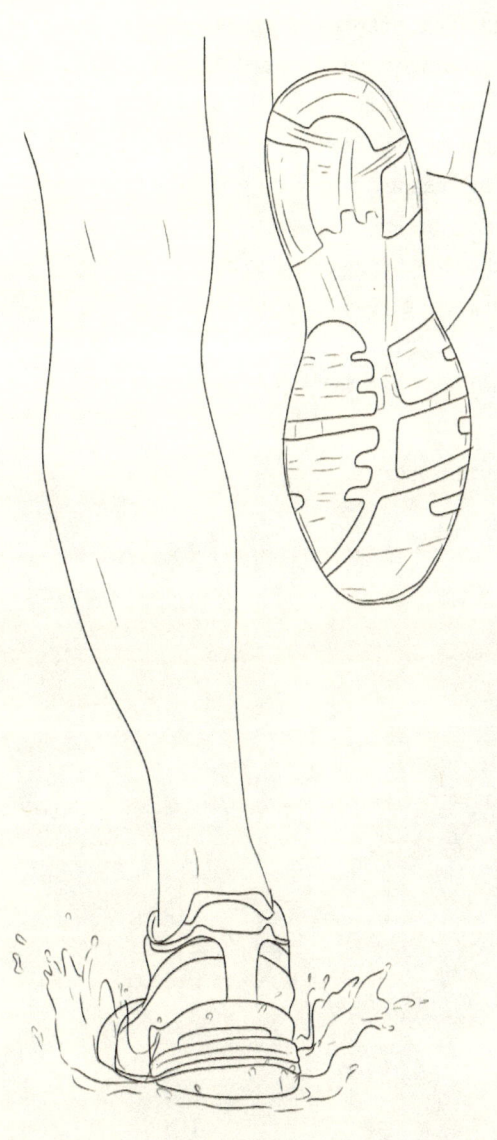

i shuffle the cards with you in mind
let's change what happened
can we pause and rewind?
show me the future
show me the cards i want to see
forget this lonely detour
get us to where we need to be
between sheets intertwined
we're together again
your body next to mine

-fortune teller

i have stars in my eyes
everything will work out
just like in the movies

you said you want me, but
we can't be together
i push that aside
you'll change your mind

you asked me on a date
said you'd play songs for me
on that old grand piano, but
you didn't show

you turned me into a fool
waiting for hours
in the auditorium
at the music school

there's been a mistake or two
it's something that will pass
like your cold glare
when i asked you how you felt and
you said, "let's not go there"

i forget the lies and
focus on the good times
like when we stole your dad's boat
and sailed it to your auntie's

let's make it a happy ending
where we end up kissing
can we do that, please?

-delulu

it's been months
since i viewed your posts online
i wonder how you're doing
i'll try not to look today
is everything falling apart
without me or
are you okay?
i'm not looking
did you get a new girlfriend?
what do you got cooking?
did you go on a trip or
get a new job?
why is it so hard not to look?
i wish i couldn't find you
i wish i could erase that chapter and
just close that book
but you're always there
all it takes is
just one click
just one look

-*always there*

you can't say for sure
you'd regret not meeting me
that's because regret will
come when it's too late
you have to wait for fate
to do its thing
something will happen
that will make you think
it'll show up in your bones
the pain in your chest
your rising stress
you'll think about what could've been
when the realization
there's no one like me
starts to set in

-regret

i'm not your mom
i won't let you
play games

i'm not your favorite barista
the pretty one you admire
over small talk and tea

i'm not your girlfriend
peace at a cost
love in a way

i'm the one who'll
put my hands into your soul
shake it awake and make it burn

-no competition

i wear glasses, but
my vision is sharp
you didn't think i'd see
straight to your heart
the parts you try to hide
i can see in plain sight
the darkness behind your eyes
tells me you wear a disguise
you run because
i'm the mirror in front you
reflecting back
who you don't want to be

-the mirror

i won't dim my light
for yours to shine brighter
i won't give you my energy again

you hurt me because
i'm a person who feels deeply
but i've moved beyond the pain

now my mind is at peace
and my body at ease
we're not kindred spirits
we were never the same

-not so kindred

you talk a good game and
know how to stoke a flame
but there's something
in your voice unspoken
whispers between words
telling me you're broken
in subtle ways, you try to
tear my heart wide open
planting seeds of doubt
to make me feel unworthy
there's no need to call you out
i can see right through you
the best thing i can do is
stay far away from you

-silence is golden

your colorful feathers are your skills
they are beautiful and
distract from what's within
i saw you as i wished you to be
but looking past your feathers
your heart is out of harmony
so harmfully careless
without apology
so painfully cold
in its philosophy

-the peacock

you didn't think i'd see you
i see you with the clarity of a flawless diamond
i see you with the clarity of a new pair of glasses
i see you with the clarity of a zero-proof cocktail
i see you more clearly than you see yourself

-in focus

when you think
with your head
not your heart
it stops us from being free
that's when my writing
drifts towards fantasy
i write about how
i want it to be
time travelers
magic and
not your everyday love
why can't we bend reality?
you focus on change and
the things in your life
you'd have to rearrange
we can build our own world
fill it with conversation and
our embrace
it's where i'm not
just someone you know
and, at best, a friend
it's where
it all works out
in the end

-unrequited

seeing your face for the first time
was like seeing a blip on the radar
in enemy waters
it was significant
i didn't know why
there was something in
the tint of your eyes
the hint of your smile
you were to play some role
slip into my soul
good or bad?
i couldn't tell
maybe you'd give me
a piece of heaven or
something closer to hell

-blip on the radar

i knew i got lost in you when
i'd fall asleep in your room
with the blinds wide open
i sleep in a room that is dark

i knew i got lost in you when
i'd pretend to have fun
at your big parties
i'd rather talk about music and art

i knew i got lost in you when
you left and i fell into the dark
my sorrow led me down a dangerous path
you almost put out my spark

i knew i had found myself when
you came to my window years later that night
i could finally see that it was always me
the light illuminating my heart

-lost and found

my love crashed into you
rolled right over you
it was heavier
than any love you knew
too big for you to fathom
i pulled you from the bottom
you got air
you got scared
it was too much for you
it happens all the time
is there anyone with a love
as big as mine?

-big love

daisy

storms came and went
changing my terrain
each one leaving
cracks in my earth
empty puddles
and pain
they tore at my leaves
and swept away seeds
love didn't grow
then you came along
there you were
a daisy in the snow

-my person

i turned the pain you gave me into beauty
you couldn't break me
i proved i have the strength and energy
to move on to a bigger destiny
i think i'm ready

-easy a

see people for who they are
not who you wish them to be
don't get caught up in the fantasy
it takes time to know a person
and understand their reality
not everyone's love is as pure as yours
save your trust until you're sure
they're not playing you for a fool

-slow down

i have a bouquet of flowers
i've plucked from pain
in the darkest of places
flowers bloom
if you look to find them

from the one who broke your heart
there waits a rose
from the one who gave you silence
there waits a lily
from the one who left you longing
there waits a lilac
from the one who disappeared
there waits a daisy

my rose gave me a new love
my lily gave me a voice
my lilac gave me peace and
my daisy gave me happiness

gather the flowers that grow and
create your beautiful bouquet
they hold precious lessons
blossoming into brighter days

-bouquet

never stop looking for the flowers
thunderstorms leave behind
trade your tears for flowers
they turn your sorrow into power

-fuck you-flowers

don't give me lukewarm love
give me the
cross-the-fifth-dimension-to-find-you
kind of love

don't give me mixed feelings
give me the
bet-it-all-on-one-number
kind of conviction

don't give me shifting energy
give me the
don't-blink-or-you'll-miss-this-once-in-a-lifetime-event
kind of attention

-what i need

you can take your eyes that you keep at a distance
your precious hands you use to make a living
your tattoos that mean something to you, and
the ones that don't

you can take your early morning messages
that greeted me with the sun
your confessions of who you are
that made me feel less alone
your shared longing for a passion
that was missing

you can take your whispers into voice messages
from your separate room
your patterns you use to create and
your almost connection

i'll keep what you can't take
the you in my art

-the artist

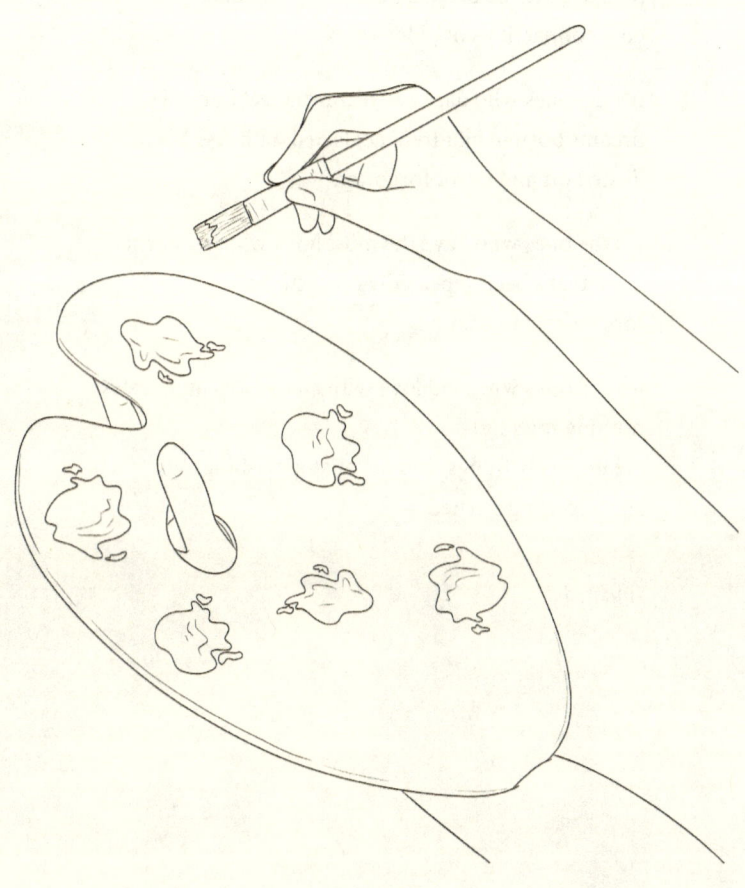

it's the ones who freely give themselves to love who get burned
love despite the broken hearts of youth and
cold connections of older years

it's the ones who dare to dream who get burned
dreams born in children, neglected with age, but
dusted off and never forgotten

it's the ones who have the most hope who get burned
hope that's been repeatedly cracked, but
forever remains intact

it's the ones who find love with all its parts and pieces
nothing missing
create lovely things, and never stop wishing
all for getting burned

-burned

are you the fit-into-the-hierarchy kind
or the cut-a-path-with-a-machete kind?
we can question what we're told
use our hearts, minds, and intuition
to pave new roads

are you the speak-the-compliant-script kind
or the pour-your-heart-into-poetry kind?
we don't have to echo the jargon
created by the few for a few
let's use our words to unite us as one

are you the profits-over-people kind
or the people-are-precious kind?
we can open our eyes to see
our hearts don't run on money
we're all units of energy fueling humanity

-for the people

my eyes store the data
my mind creates the narrative
my heart holds the profits
my fingers type the messages
i'm always working
i'm always home
i am my home

-wfh

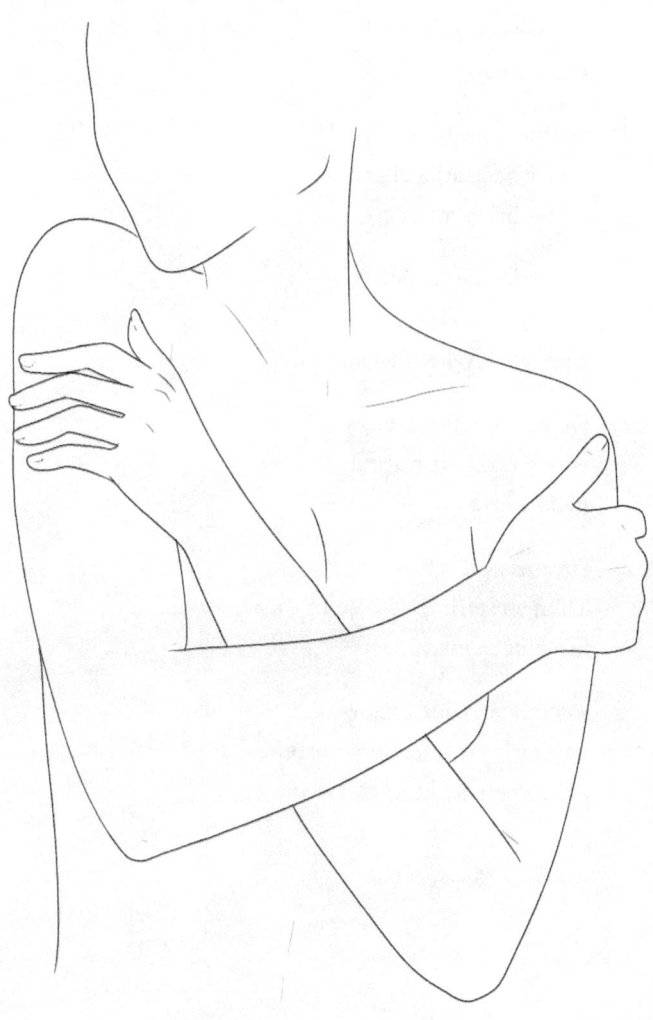

i don't always choose
the perfect words and
put them in perfect places

my love may be messy
it may be irrational and
it may bring me pain

i'm not AI perfection
with all its answers
a perfect loveless machine

i'm an imperfect human
with human poems and
human love

i'm energy in a body
a human spirit
in a human machine

sometimes, i don't know what to say, but
i promise my intentions are pure
even when my heart gets in the way

-spirit in the machine

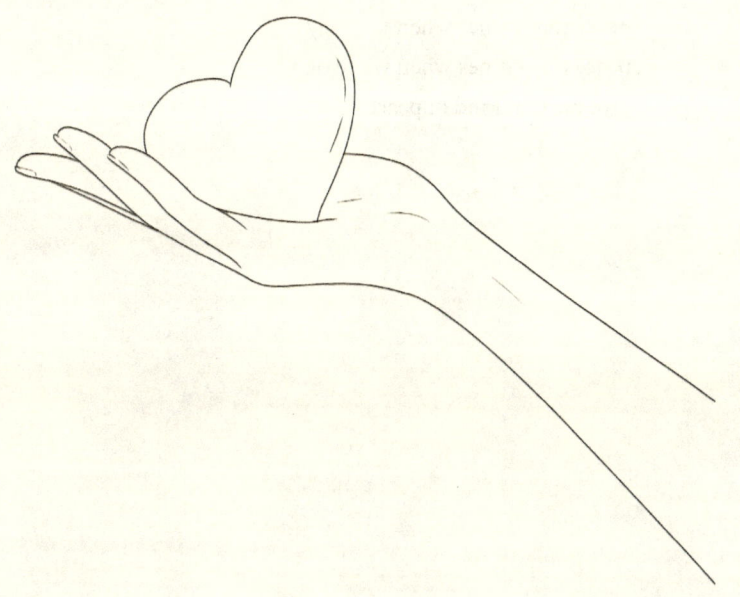

i don't want a boring peace
i want a passionate peace
peace when you tell me how you feel
even if it's hard to hear
peace when you push past the fear of what you'll lose
because it's better to feel
peace that comes when you stay
peace that comes when we're one
give me that kind of peace

-my kind of peace

love hurts
but i can't help it
i'll jump in again

it took too long to heal
to stop thinking about you
first thing in the morning
every night before bed
when i think of things you said
long after the last message you left

love hurts
but it feels too good
to not love again

-running jump

expressing my hurt
does not make me weak
so what if i cried?
i asked if you cared
and you stared at me
tongue-tied
you pushed away feeling
but feeling is strength
letting love in
being vulnerable
opening up
expressing
communicating
honesty and
authenticity
shows true power
i'm happy it's over
someone's looking for me
and he's a bold lover

-power in feeling

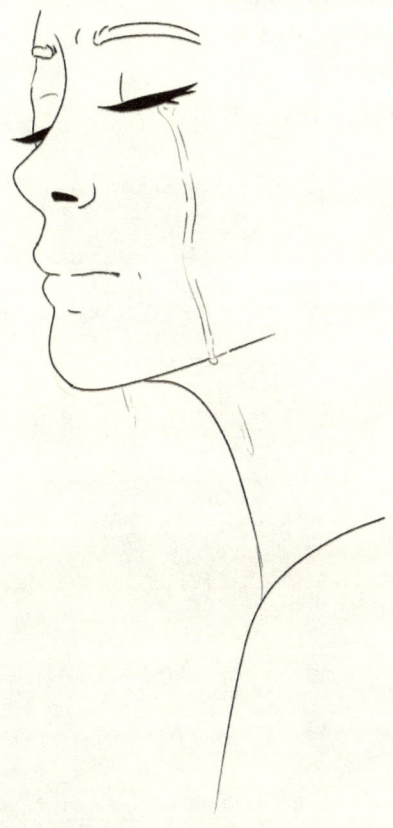

i'd rather have tried and
had you break my heart
than to let my days slip by
without the kind of love
that makes life worthwhile

-*worth the risk*

if i don't find you in this life
i won't shed too many tears
i'll find you on the other side
at the end of my earthly years

-*immortals*

her light attracts
but the intensity
makes some people step back
they close their eyes
she reflects back the lies
they tell themselves to get by
she illuminates the void within them
they rather be numb
scared of what they'll see
they run from her authenticity
for they wear a façade
to fit in with the crowd
but there are some
who don't hide out
they step into her light
they lift people up and
change their lives

-the sun

love is now a challenge i take on gladly
i dare you to break my heart
i'll get over it

but until then
i'll swim in the sadness a bit

the water is welcoming and warm
like an old friend

until i'm caught in someone else's storm
i'll wade into the deep end

i like to swim
love will find me again

-swimmer

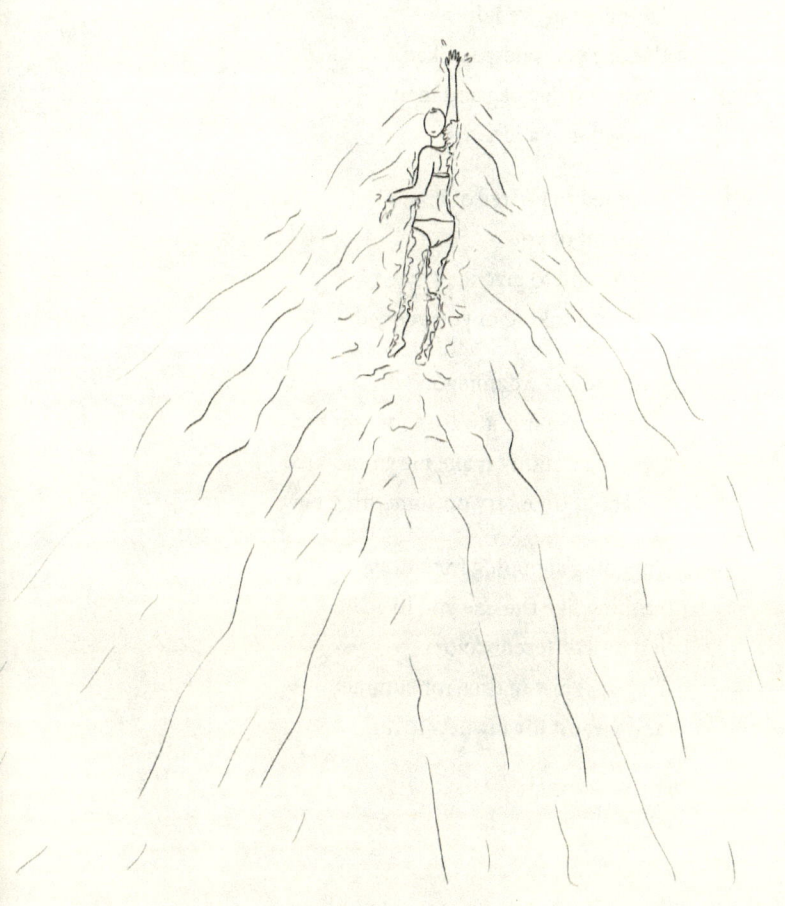

i donated my red dress
the one you said you liked
i tossed it in a bag and then
i tossed it in a bin

i wanted to be free of it and
every bit of you
it felt good to give it away
to stop thinking of you every day

but that was a damn good dress
i'd still have it if it wasn't for you and
wearing it didn't make me so sad
it's about time i try on something new

i'm going shopping for a dress
nothing like the one you liked
it'll be a different color
i'll buy it just in time for summer
and wear it for my new lover

-new dress

don't let the people
who don't deserve your energy
take it from you
wish them on their way and
wish them well
use your energy wisely
share it with the worthy
you have poems to write
you have stories to tell

-note to self

you make me feel special
like i'm the only one
of course
it feels great but
then you manipulate
you shift your energy
i don't feel safe
so i'll take back
my attention and time
protect my own energy and
bid you goodbye

-self-care

i went into our chat and
deleted every message i sent you
just like that
i took back everything i gave you
i took back the pieces of me
my thoughts and words
you don't deserve
with every message i deleted
i felt less depleted by you
i'll take my words and start anew
i'll give them to someone
who's worthy and true

-*reclamation*

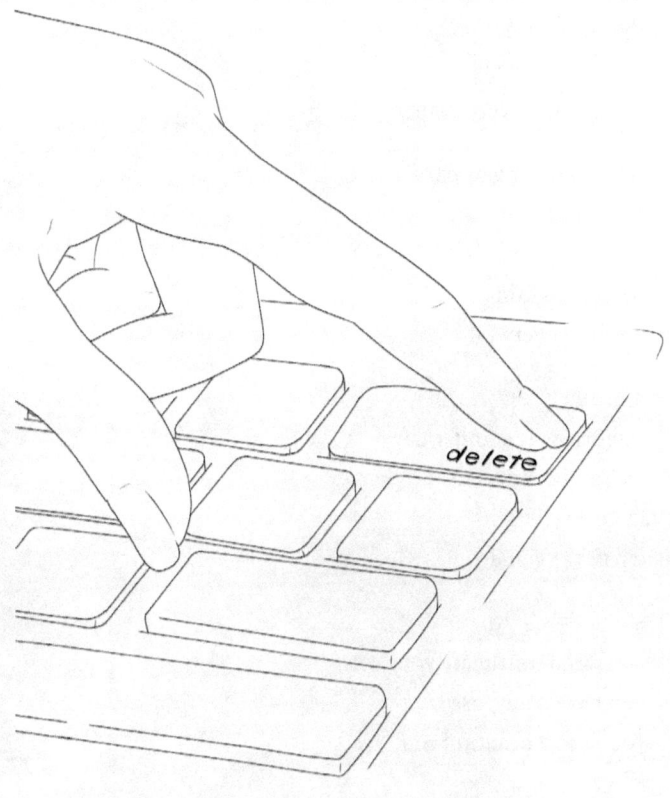

i know it's dark
don't dim your light
the world needs you
tomorrow, today
tonight and every night

sometimes, it gets hard
don't quit
we need your grit
so keep fighting
we need every bit

don't go
tomorrow is another day
we're all connected
in unseen ways
whatever you do
just stay

don't underestimate your role
you have a purpose
you have a beautiful soul

just remember
we're all in this together

-beautiful souls

if they're a dense fog and
always leave you questioning
their feelings for you

if they're a dark cloud and
always leave you confused
about their intentions

if they're an overcast day and
always leave you wondering
whether they love you

it's time to
let the hurt pass through
like a rainstorm that
cries with you
washes you clean
waters your seeds

it's time to
move into a new future
one with endless possibilities
flowers to bloom
surprises to come and
skies that are clear

-sunny with a chance of daisies

tough times are like
thunderstorms
they come and go
so just know
that if you're in a bad storm
blue skies are on the horizon
soon, there will be a time when
the light breaks through the clouds
and the sun will shine

-sunny skies ahead

you think you're
a ship in the storm
your sails torn
waves consume you

you think you're
dangerous to chase
you keep running
fear drives you

you think you're
a train wreck
your metal twisted
your tracks broken

look closer
you're a sail in the calm
your waters still
your skies cloudless

look closer
you're a stroll through the park
your temperature warm
your flowers in bloom

look closer
you're a ride on a bullet train
fast but steady
a silent lullaby

shift your perspective and
look past your heartache
see yourself as i see you
you're not your bad experiences
you're not your mistakes

-look closer

you smile for the camera
you put on a show
you laugh and
your eyes glow

alone in your den
your eyes turn red and
you're met by the demons
in your head

your den is decorated with
curtains of bad memories
walls painted in anxiety
floors covered in fear and
doors to keep out the ones
who hold you dear

you're not a bad witch
you're a good witch
locked in a den
who needs to let
love in again

-*good witch*

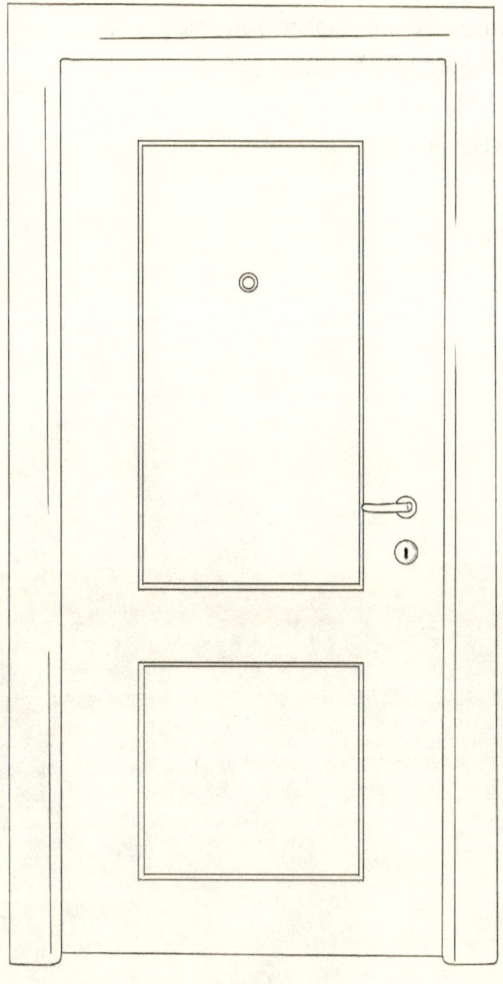

solitude is where we plant our flowers
it's where we contemplate their true power
don't be afraid to be alone
our bodies are our home
it's where we create love on our own

-solitude

i have a thing for love songs
i put on rose-tinted glasses and sing along
but no one wrote a song for me
my hazel eyes and honest smile
aren't etched into notes
all because someone loves me

i want to be a character in a book
i'm the protagonist who falls in love
after just one look
but there's concrete under my feet
dreams exist only when i sleep
no one wrote me into any story

i haven't found my way into a poem
maybe i'm not made for them
my cleopatra gaze and
voice that captivates
aren't woven into verse or meter
i don't live in anyone's poetry

there's no shining knight with a pen
it's my keyboard and
my words on the other end
i'm the songwriter
storyteller and
poet

-always the poet

a lady with visions and guides
told me a person
would come into my life
all my dreams personified
in about a year, she said
i looked at her and laughed
now, i can't help but wonder
who will he be?
i asked her about another
she said no, it's not him
he's playing a game
that man's light is dim
now, i can't help but wonder
what color are his eyes?
will he make my heart roar
like the thunder that tore
through here last night?
what is he like?
will he make me laugh until
my belly aches and
my eyes tear?
i can't wait to meet him but
i have to wait another year
as long as it takes
that's how long i'll wait
his face a mystery
just like his smile
for now, it's a surprise
until we're reflections
in each other's eyes

-supernatural

do you dream?
i'm not talking about
the future you want
places you'd like to see or
the person you wish to be

do you dream?
in the middle of the night
when visions fill your head
a way to see without sight
things you wouldn't see
in the daylight

when i'm fast asleep
it's when energies meet
the messages in the dark
ignite a spark in me
we can make our dreams reality

-i dream

we talked about energy and
what's beyond life
we sent messages from our phones but
it felt like you were right next to me
you made me feel less alone

we talked about the things we did
others in our shoes wouldn't do
you told me a story about you
i painted a picture of it in my mind
if i was there with you
i'd run in the mud with you
i swear you're my kind

we talked about the things we want
to know each other
kiss and be close
you had a dream about me and
i dreamed about you the same night
our energies unite
just in that place and
on that one night

-energies unite

do you quietly flicker or
do you burn with intensity?

do you hide within the crowd
so no one sees?

do you get by and
live your life carefully?

or do you
takes chances
climb mountains
swim against currents
scream
rage
dance
laugh
love?

do you live spectacularly?

-make it spectacular

when i step out of myself
look at my world from a far-off moon
i don't think about
the price tag on my homes
my degrees that have gathered dust or
job titles i've rattled off in conversation

the things i think about are
the people i love
the way i felt when i first saw you
getting stuck in your eyes a moment too long
when you couldn't look away

in the end
all that will matter is
the energy
the love
the connection

-what matters

every time we talked, another piece of you sunk into my soul
your voice became the song on repeat
your eyes became a morning cup of coffee
your hands became my favorite clothes
your body became the moment before slipping into a dream
there will always be some version of you lost within me

-versions

i hope that one day, you wake up and
the morning sun will give you clarity
that its light and warmth will tell you a story
that will set you on your next journey
i hope that one day you'll be free

i hope that one day, you find your way
out of all the uncertainty
that feeling of whether to take your things and leave
let go of everything heavy
i hope that one day you'll be free

i hope that one day, you see a new world
with your place in it that makes you happy
that space with puppy hugs
windows that let in lots of light
lattes on ice and cakes topped with honey
i hope that one day you'll be free

i hope that one day, you'll find someone and
allow yourself to fall into their gravity
that someone who will get excited
about what you create
be late to kiss you over coffee
i hope that one day you'll be free

even if it's not with me
i hope that one day you'll be free

-free like me

if i could hold time in my hands
i'd smoosh it into a ball and
stretch it out like dough to find you

you're sticky
stretched thin
you fit into a cookie-cutter
i take your shape

save you as the best part
bake you into my memory
this time
we make a new start

i eat you whole
you're soft and sweet
you're mine
you're mine
you're mine
we dream in endless sleep

-time cookie

don't fall to your knees for me
every time
fall to your knees for me
sometimes
there has to be
sometimes
when you fall
i'll fall too
i'll do whatever
you want me to

-partnership of equals

you were in the frame
but i put the camera down
like in the movie we talked about

that moment
and you
every moment
with you

no video can capture you
no photograph can capture you
not like i do

-in the moment

meet me in tokyo
we'll set the place on fire
our hearts will beat to taiko

meet me in positano
we'll set the place on fire
turning heads in the grotto

meet me on my patio in sacramento
we don't have to go far
we'll talk about who we were years ago

as long as i'm with you
we'll set the place on fire
wherever we go

we'll burn so bright
we'll create our own northern lights
we'll turn the night skies indigo

-doesn't matter where

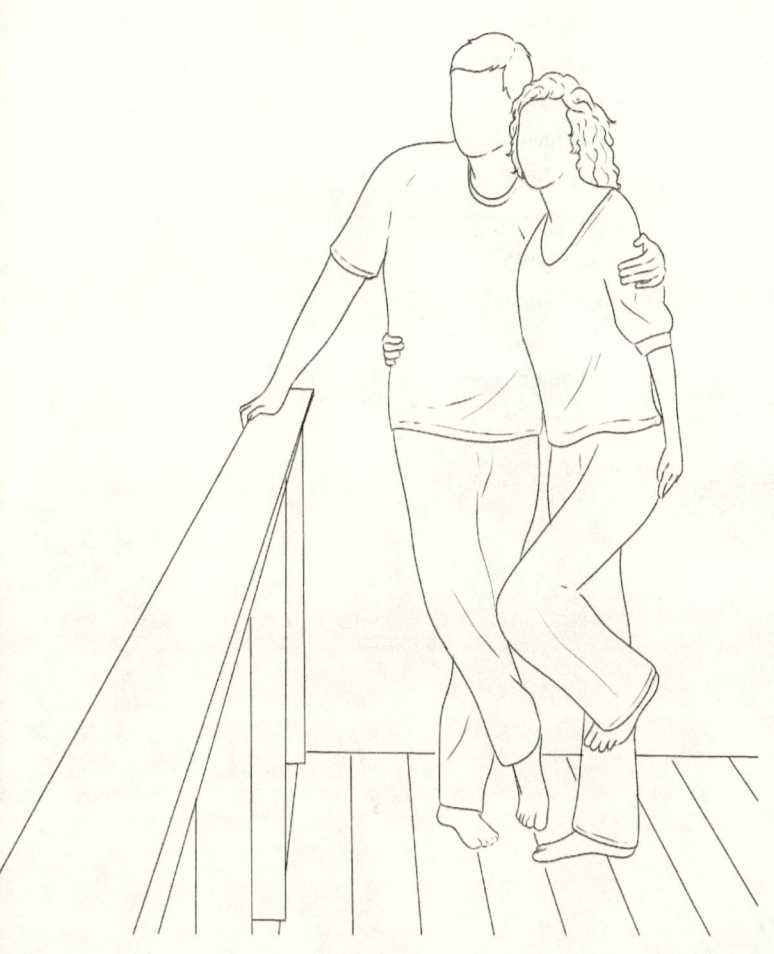

i'll be honey on your fingers
your sticky and sweet
if i'm your only storm
you don't have to ask me twice
i'll be your flame in the candle
your lonely heart waiting to meet
if i'm your daisy
i'll love you now
i'll love you tomorrow
i'll love you on repeat

-*exclusive*

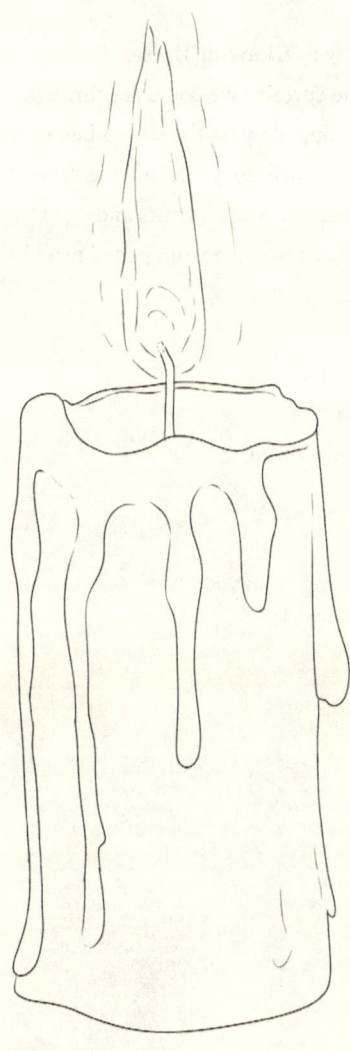

at the window overlooking the sea
tangled in the curtains we could see through so clearly
motorcycles zipped by on the streets below and
we could hear music coming from the downstairs bistro
you stole a kiss that wasn't yours and
i kissed you back because you opened new doors
my head spun
i got dizzy
i couldn't feel the floor
with that one kiss
all i wanted was more

-game over

if you want to
touch me
my skin
my curves

if you want to
kiss me
my mouth
my soul

first, you must try
your key
in the lock of
my mind

if it fits and
unlocks
there's a burning blaze
inside

-love lock

you didn't have to tell me you liked my red dress
the reflection of it burned in your eyes like fire

you didn't have to tell me the things you wished for
the desire was written into the story on your face

you didn't have to tell me you wanted to kiss me
the need was etched into the corners of your mouth

-red dress

your voice is an immeasurable pleasure
it's a spell, a lullaby, and an adventure

your voice is the sound of love
it's the song i want to write and have been dreaming of

your voice is the passion building within
it's what i tell myself will wash away all the sin

-secrets

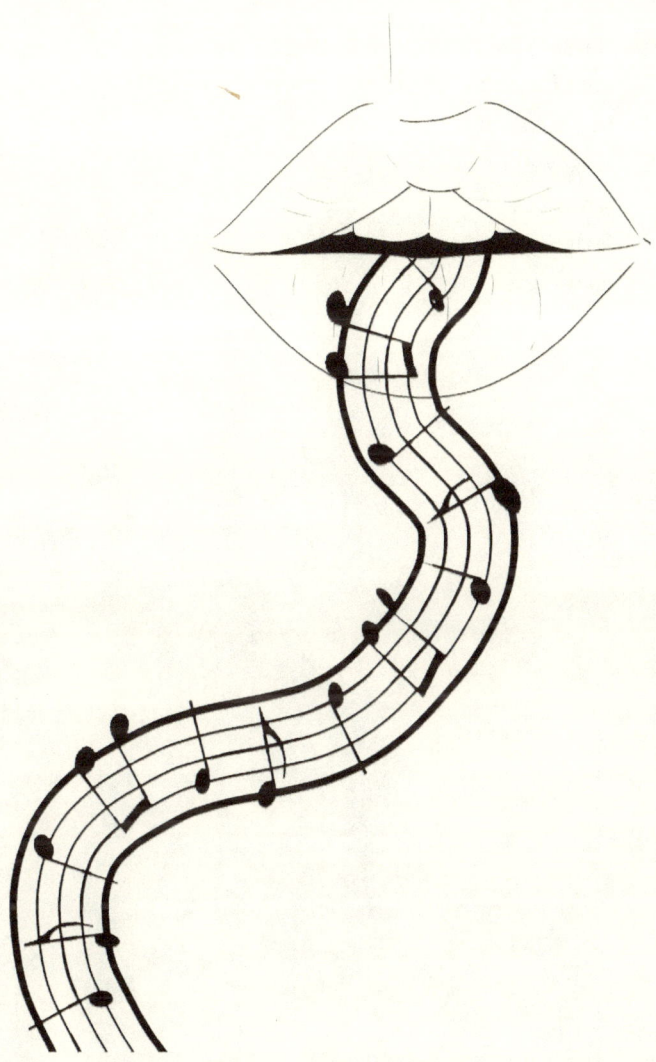

the words
"i want you"
are a flickering flame
in a candle but
what we say
with our eyes
is the sun blazing
between us

-hush

the touch of your hand is quicksand
i couldn't leave you if i tried
there goes my control
now, it's just us and
you're the guide
i'm a writer without a pen
you write the script
you decide

-caught in you

within your eyes, i'm alive
you're witness to my being
your gaze erases all my crimes
i forget the times i've been
untrusting, defensive, and unkind
i'm not pixels on a screen
i'm a human being
who's never felt so seen
your gaze reminds me of a spirit's
the one who came to me when dreaming
he crossed eternal bridges and
loved me without limit

-brought to life

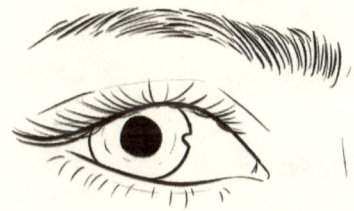
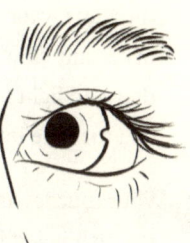

your whispers and
the breaths between them
create words in my head
i arrange them into stories
you turn me into a love poem

your kisses and
the way i want more
makes my skin glow
they add light to my life
you turn me into a sparkling gem

your touches and
the feeling left by them
makes me tall
they color my cheeks
you turn me into a rose on a long stem

-things you turn me into

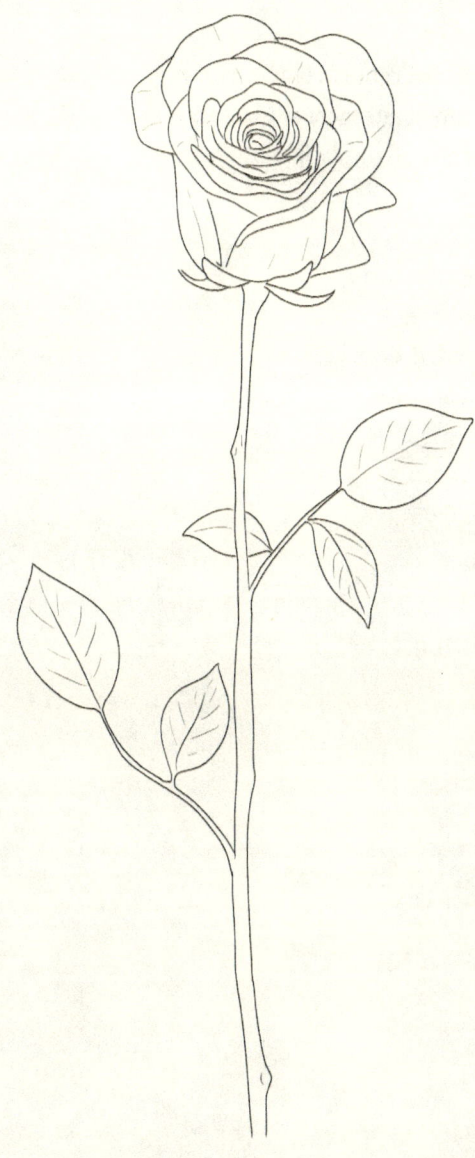

our hearts beat to the same pattern
your love lights the way like a lantern
and erases all the dark in my heart
your words soothe my soul
with you
i have no control
in your eyes
there are firecrackers
that flicker when i look in them
and i
burn
burn
burn

-masterful

thank you for reading *thunder and daisy*. i hope it resonated with you. following this book, my debut novel will be released, and it will include a reference to *thunder and daisy*. as you read my books, you'll be able to uncover links between them. i'd love for you to join me on this journey.

it would also mean the world to me if you could take a moment to review *thunder and daisy* where you purchased it. your reviews make a big difference and help other readers discover my work.

-a thank you note from me to you

MERCEDES PARADISO is a poet and author. though she also has a background as an attorney, she feels most herself when writing poems and novels. her work explores the struggles and beauty of the human condition. mercedes loves crafting poems and stories and spending time with family. to learn more about mercedes and stay updated on her books, visit her on instagram @mzparadiso and her website mercedesparadiso.com.

-a note about the author